LIFE

THE BEATLES
They're here again
and what a ruckus!

W
What in the World?
W

AUGUST 28 · 1964 · 25¢

The Beatles:
Sgt. Pepper's Lonely Hearts Club Band

Teresa Wimmer

Creative Education
an imprint of The Creative Company

Introduction

On a spring day in 1967, the four members of the Beatles gathered around the recording equipment in their London studio. They were listening critically to the last song on their latest album. As the final, gasping piano chord reverberated for nearly a minute before the record player screeched to a halt, the Beatles shook their heads. It needed something more. They rushed onto the studio floor to record themselves making funny noises and chanting "Never could be any other way," then looped the statement to repeat endlessly. With that, *Sgt. Pepper's Lonely Hearts Club Band* was complete, and there would never be any other like it.

In 1960, Sirimavo Bandaranaike became prime minister of Sri Lanka (formerly Ceylon), the first woman elected prime minister of any country. During her three terms, she worked to make Sri Lanka a republic.

Sirimavo Bandaranaike finished her first term as prime minister in 1965 and was re-elected in 1970.

In May 1967, the Beatles celebrated the recent release of their new album Sgt. Pepper's Lonely Hearts Club Band.

The Berlin Wall, separating communist East Germany from democratic West Germany, was a powerful symbol of the Cold War era.

A Time for Change

The road that led to the making of one of rock music's most influential albums began in 1966 in a world consumed by political and social upheaval. After the capitalist United States and the communist Soviet Union emerged from World War II as the world's undisputed superpowers, they spent the next 40 years in continual opposition with each other. The two nations engaged in a

In 1961, President John F. Kennedy created the Peace Corps to provide humanitarian aid to foreign countries. The program drew many young people who were eager to donate two years of their lives to peaceful service.

"Cold War" that was marked by threats and antagonism but never erupted in all-out combat—at least not in those countries.

In the late 1950s, U.S. President Dwight Eisenhower pledged small amounts of aid to South Vietnam in its struggle against communist North Vietnam. That soon escalated into a commitment to station hundreds of thousands of American troops

While president, John F. Kennedy dealt with many tense situations related to the potential use of nuclear weapons.

in Vietnam by 1967. Many people, especially youth, in the U.S. and around the world grew increasingly opposed to the Vietnam War, and sit-ins and draft dodging became common forms of protest. The rebellion against and violence of the drawn-out war, which would not end until 1975, came to characterize the decade of the 1960s.

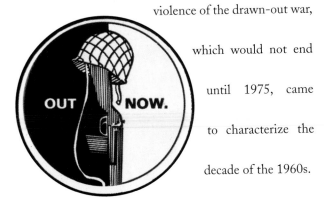

In addition to the political tensions of the Cold War, the era was also defined by the struggle for racial equality. In South Africa, apartheid, a system by which the white minority controlled the government and oppressed the black majority, had been in place since 1948, but it came to the world's attention in 1963. That year, black activist Nelson Mandela was jailed for sabotage, organizing guerilla forces, and refusing to obey the laws of a white parliament

Those opposed to the Vietnam War demonstrated openly and wore buttons proclaiming their sentiments (above).

Soviet cosmonaut Yuri Gagarin (pictured) became the first person in space in 1961. In response, President John F. Kennedy declared that the U.S. would put a man on the moon by the decade's end.

Nelson Mandela was first jailed in 1962 but received a harsher sentence of life in prison the following year.

Claes Oldenburg's unorthodox statues, such as this one in Seoul, South Korea, are found all over the world.

in which he was not represented. He remained incarcerated for the next 27 years and gained worldwide support for the dignity and courage he exhibited in his attempts to correct social injustices and unite his nation.

To counterbalance the social strife, a feeling of optimism brought about by technological advancements permeated the decade. The '60s saw the first cochlear implant to help deaf people hear and the first measles vaccine. In 1963, Soviet textile worker Valentina Tereshkova became the first woman in space, and six years later, the U.S. launched the *Apollo 11* lunar mission. Millions of TV viewers watched as astronauts Neil Armstrong and Edwin "Buzz" Aldrin hosted a live TV broadcast from the surface of the moon.

Prompted by the unconventional times and enlightened by the existentialist ideas of French writers such as Jean-Paul Sartre and Albert Camus, artists explored new mediums for expressing the meaning and absurdity of everyday life. Experimental theater groups in the U.S., Europe, and Japan featured stripped-down plays that required few props. Pop artists such as Andy Warhol and Claes Oldenburg challenged people's concepts of art by using consumer goods such as soup cans and lipstick tubes in their works. And Beat authors such as Jack Kerouac and Allen Ginsberg opened minds to alternative lifestyles and altered forms of consciousness.

Such mind-broadening ideas led young people around the world to reject the traditional values of their dominant culture, or "The Establishment." In Poland and Yugoslavia, students protested restrictions on free speech imposed by communist regimes. Members of the British countercultural movement strove to break down class barriers so that the working class could achieve some degree of wealth and higher education. Some young people became hippies and advocated their values of peace, free love, communalism, and individuality.

Disoriented young people looked for a means of self-expression and a feeling of togetherness. They found both in the music of American folk-rock singers such as Bob Dylan and Joan Baez and French rock idol Johnny Hallyday. Such groundbreaking artists then paved the way for a group of four musicians from Liverpool, England, called the Beatles, to tap into the counterculture movement, use it to expand their creativity, and ultimately become its leaders.

In 1963, Kenya gained its independence from Great Britain. As the decade progressed, many other African countries broke free of colonial rule, further diminishing the influence of the once vast British Empire.

Artists such as folk-rock icons Bob Dylan and Joan Baez (left) and feminist writer Gloria Steinem (opposite, left) urged social change.

American author and feminist Betty Friedan published *The Feminine Mystique* in 1963. The best seller helped trigger the 20th century's second push toward equal rights for women, known as the Women's Liberation Movement.

Beatlemania and Beyond

John Lennon, Paul McCartney, George Harrison, and Ringo Starr—who would later be known as the Beatles—were all born to middle-class families in Liverpool, England. They came of age in the countercultural atmosphere of the 1960s, experiencing personal and artistic quests for understanding along with the rest of their generation.

John Lennon was born in 1940 and raised primarily by his aunt and uncle. As a teenager, Lennon shunned authority figures, listening instead to American rock 'n' roll radio broadcasts. He learned how to play the guitar and dreamed of making such wild and free music as his idol, Elvis Presley. In late 1956, the 16-year-old formed his first band, called The Quarry Men, which led to his first meeting with Paul McCartney.

In the mid-1960s, the Twist, the Frug, the Monkey, and the Watusi became the rage on dance floors across the U.S. and Europe. The free-form dances reflected the era's rejection of 1950s conservatism.

The Twist dance was born when a song by the same name was recorded by singer Chubby Checker in 1960.

In their early years, the young, clean-shaven members of the Beatles projected a happy, carefree image.

McCartney was a polite, well-spoken, but mischievous child whose mother, Mary, often read poetry to him. Like Lennon, McCartney listened to radio broadcasts of American rock music and learned to play the guitar as a teenager. When his mother died of cancer in 1956, McCartney dealt with his grief by playing his guitar. A year later, McCartney met Lennon after one of The Quarry Men's concerts at a church fundraiser and impressed the lead singer so much that Lennon asked him to join them.

George Harrison knew Paul McCartney from their daily rides on the school bus, but it wasn't until he learned how to play guitar as a teenager that Harrison thought anything of it. While riding the bus one day, Harrison and McCartney discovered their mutual love of rock music. In 1958, McCartney introduced Harrison to Lennon, who saw potential in Harrison and asked him to join The Quarry Men.

John Lennon, pictured around 1961.

From 1965 to 1970, Communist prime minister Fidel Castro allowed thousands of Cubans to emigrate to the U.S. because of a severe housing crisis in Cuba.

The first miniskirt was sighted in London near the end of 1965. It soon became one of the most influential fashion trends in many countries, maintaining its popularity throughout the rest of the century.

Changing the band's name to "the Silver Beetles," which was then shortened to "the Beatles," McCartney, Lennon, and Harrison realized they needed more than a new name—there was still one member missing.

Ringo Starr (whose birth name was Richard Starkey) had a childhood plagued by illness. During one of his recoveries at a children's hospital, he discovered his natural drum-playing ability. After working a few menial jobs as a young adult, Starr turned back to drumming. Through word of mouth, the Beatles learned of Starr's ability and, in 1962, asked him to join the band.

Before he joined the Beatles, Ringo Starr was a drummer for Rory Storm and the Hurricanes.

Thurgood Marshall (pictured, center) was sworn in as the 96th U.S. Supreme Court justice in 1967. The great-grandson of a slave, Marshall was most known for his decisions in favor of civil rights.

The Beatles guest-starred on such popular British TV programs as the Ken Dodd Show *before touring the world.*

After the failed experiment of the Prague Spring, citizens of the city of Prague protested the occupation of the Soviets.

The Beatles' most adoring fans were young women.

Like most young musicians, the foursome at first played anywhere in England they could get paid—at parks, clubs, and everywhere in between. With the release of the single "Please Please Me" in 1963, the rest of Europe discovered the "Fab Four." Europeans were hooked by the Beatles' irresistible blend of catchy melodies, close harmonies, nimble guitar pickings, and dynamic chords. In only a year's time, the mop-haired, black-suited young men found themselves playing songs such as "I Want to Hold Your Hand" to concert halls filled with throngs of screaming teenage girls. The Beatles' rapid

Television host Ed Sullivan (center) proudly introduced the Beatles to American audiences in 1964.

ascent was unlike anything England had ever seen, and the press dubbed the phenomenon "Beatlemania."

When the Beatles landed in New York in February 1964 to begin a tour of the U.S., they were greeted by thousands of enthusiastic fans. Their wit, charm, infectious music, and appearances on the *Ed Sullivan Show* made the Beatles even bigger stars in America than they had been in Europe. Their music excited a generation yearning to break free of the conservatism and repression of the post-war 1950s, and they became hip role models for the restless youth who came of age during the 1960s.

The summer of 1967 is often called the "Summer of Love" for its promotion that peace and love would conquer all. *Sgt. Pepper*'s theme of the need for universal love helped define that summer.

The idea for the Beatles' name originated from the band Buddy Holly and the Crickets (pictured), whose music excited the Beatles, and was a reference to the avant-garde Beat poets and musicians of the 1950s.

American Jasper Johns' work revolutionized art in the 1960s.

Yet, as the decade wore on, the Beatles discovered they would have to change their music to reflect the times if they wanted to maintain their influence on music and society. The counterculture's emphasis on artistic and social experimentation had turned the world upside down by 1965. Ever the inventive artists, the Beatles moved away from the teen love songs that characterized the Beatlemania period and followed in the footsteps of protest singers such as Bob Dylan and the introspective Janis Joplin. The group was challenged emotionally and creatively as it worked toward achieving a more complex and intellectual style.

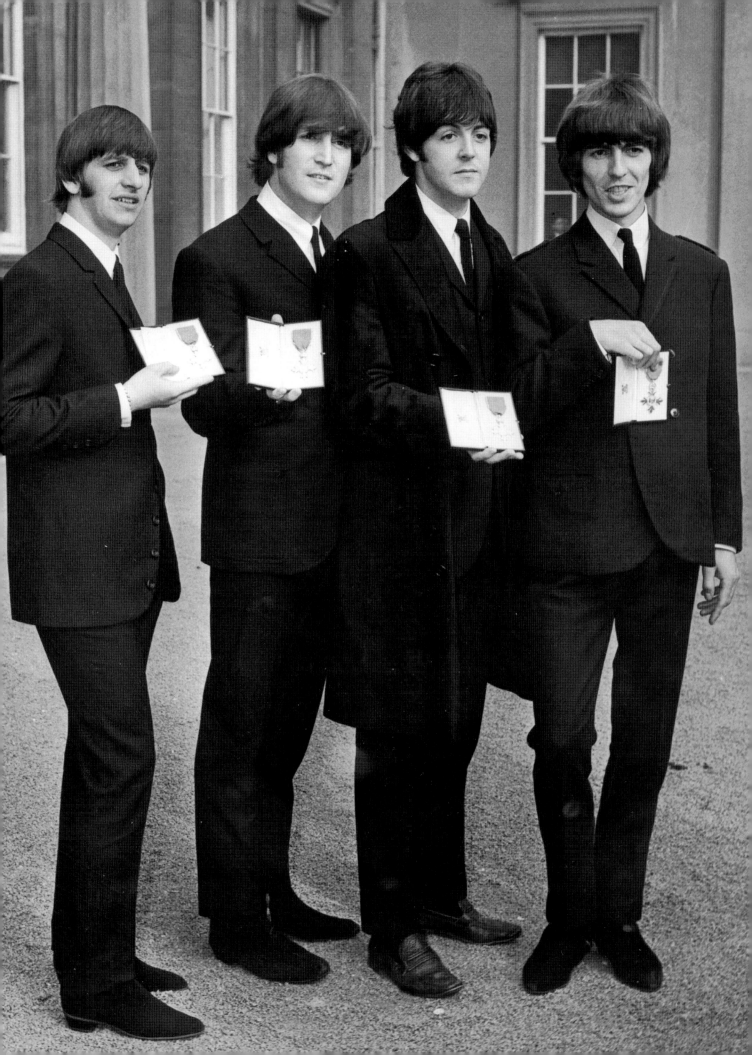

John Lennon's first child, Julian (center), was five years old when Lennon married second wife Yoko Ono in 1968.

On January 12, 1964, the Beatles played at the famous London Palladium theater before embarking on a world tour.

John Lennon's mother Julia died when John was 18. Julia had been more of a friend than a parent to Lennon, but the loss still had a profound impact on him. He named his first child, Julian, after her.

Ringo Starr's steady beat and nearly perfect sense of tempo allowed the Beatles to record songs many times and edit the versions together to make the best song. Today, most bands use a metronome to keep time.

With *Rubber Soul* (1965) and *Revolver* (1966), two albums released to critical and commercial success, the Beatles showed the world what they were capable of. The songs on these albums, though still written by Lennon and McCartney, were different from anything they had done before. They were the artistic products of adults who were reflecting on their world. The albums began to change the image of the Beatles from teen idols to cultural revolutionaries. However, it would be the Beatles' next album that would cement their iconic status and alter the course of rock music forever.

Rubber Soul, *the Beatles' sixth album, was written in a hurry but shows the influence of contemporaries such as Bob Dylan.*

Sgt. Pepper and His Band

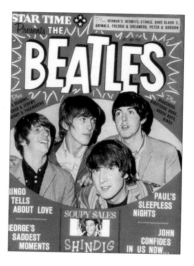

By 1966, the Beatles had grown tired of the Beatlemania craze and of the constant mobs wherever they went. All four members took time to travel the world separately. In October, McCartney returned to England from a vacation in Kenya. While on the plane, he got an idea for an album featuring a fictional

The Beatles released the song "Yesterday" in 1965. The lyrical, intimate ballad became the most covered song of all time, with more than 3,000 versions by artists as varied as Ray Charles and Placido Domingo.

band. The four Beatles would all assume the roles of members of an act called the Sgt. Pepper's Lonely Hearts Club Band. The name of the band itself was derived from a play on the words "salt" and "pepper."

Back in England, though, McCartney had a harder time convincing the other band

From posters for sale on London's Portobello Road (opposite) to magazine covers, images of the Beatles were everywhere.

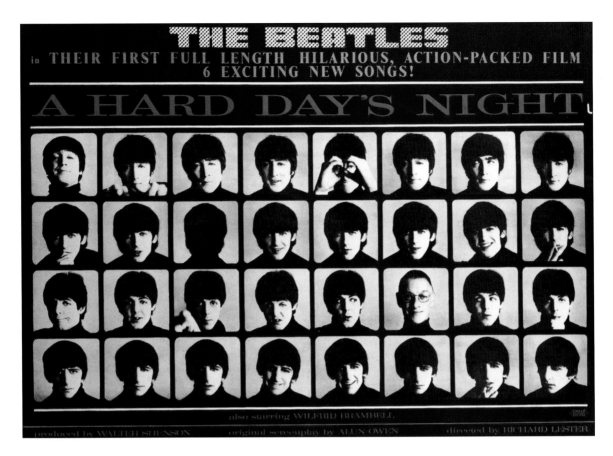

Between making their first film in 1964 (above) and releasing Sgt. Pepper *in 1967, the Beatles evolved as a band.*

In 1967, the Beatles formed Apple Corps Ltd., which encompassed business ventures such as the Apple record label. Its executives later sued the computer company Apple Inc. for exclusive rights to the Apple brand name.

PADDINGTON STREET. W.1.

apple

members that doing a concept album was a good idea. Lennon and Harrison were especially wary of what they perceived as a gimmick, the idea of playing as members of a fictitious band. However, since they had stopped touring, the three had had time to write new songs, and they realized they had almost enough material for an album already. So, with all four Beatles on board, *Sgt. Pepper's Lonely Hearts Club Band* began production in late 1966.

From the beginning, it was apparent that *Sgt. Pepper* would be unlike anything that had come before it. Over the course of five months, the Beatles experimented with different sounds and re-recorded songs until they were perfect. They spent $5,500 on the album's cover art alone and tinkered with creating a concert atmosphere without live concert recordings. They did this by using studio sounds such as whistles, pipe organs, orchestral sounds played backwards, Indian sitar music, the amplified sound of combs on cardboard toilet paper tubes, and high-pitched sounds that only dogs could hear.

In 1966, the American magazine *Datebook* published an interview in which John Lennon declared that the Beatles were "more popular than Jesus." In protest, some conservative Christians held bonfires to burn Beatles albums.

A show celebrating the unity of a world newly connected by 31 communication satellites was broadcast from the Beatles' London studio in 1967. Among other songs, the Beatles performed "All You Need Is Love."

The Beatles were later portrayed by modern artists such as Andy Warhol (above) and made into collectible dolls (below).

By the time *Sgt. Pepper* was recorded, the Beatles had discovered how drugs, especially marijuana and LSD, or acid, could influence their music. The out-of-mind feelings they experienced while on an acid trip led to the creation of songs, some people said, that could best be understood by listeners who were also high. Others would later contend that,

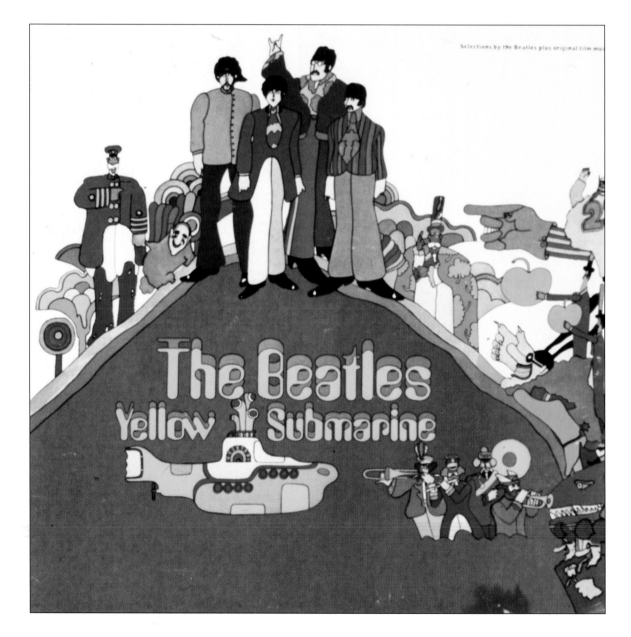

The Beatles' 1968 film Yellow Submarine *is set in a mythical paradise under the sea called Pepperland.*

The Beatles acted out their parts in Sgt. Pepper's Lonely Hearts Club Band.

The Apple Scruffs was a small group of British teenage girls who gathered outside the Beatles' homes, followed them to their Apple headquarters and studio, then waited for hours to follow them home.

despite psychedelic imagery and allusions, songs such as "Lucy in the Sky with Diamonds" and "Being for the Benefit of Mr. Kite" were inspired by purely physical sources. The Beatles maintained that "Lucy in the Sky with Diamonds" came from a painting done by Lennon's four-year-old son, Julian, and the kaleidoscope of electronic, otherworldly sounds represented the boy's artwork rather than the singer's altered state of consciousness.

Although he had an easygoing, unassuming personality, Ringo Starr loved to wear flashy rings on his fingers. The leader of the band he was in before the Beatles nicknamed him "Ringo" for that very reason.

The *Sgt. Pepper* cover featured pictures of such famous people as actress Marilyn Monroe, philosopher Karl Marx, author H. G. Wells, and boxer Sonny Liston. Adolf Hitler had originally been included but was later removed.

Released on June 1, 1967, *Sgt. Pepper* broke new ground in other ways. It was rock's first concept album, in which many of the songs had a common theme—prevalent in today's rock music but a novel idea at the time. The album opens with Starr, as fictional singer Billy Shears, inviting listeners to come in and enjoy the show. Though perhaps only two songs—the title song "Sgt. Pepper's Lonely Hearts Club Band" and "With a Little Help from My Friends"—keep to the album's original notion of the Beatles portraying fictional characters, the album is unified by the theme of duality, the idea of being "inside" and "outside," in reality and in a dream world, at the same time. Songs such as "Within You Without You,"

In 2007, Britain celebrated the 50th anniversary of Lennon and McCartney's first meeting with special stamps.

The 1968 TV broadcast of a full-length Beatles concert (above) did not require tickets.

featuring Harrison's sitar music and Eastern philosophical lyrics, and "Fixing a Hole"

exemplify this theme. The clash of various sounds at the end of "A Day in the Life"

closes the album with a celebration of sorts, as if signaling the end of Sgt. Pepper's,

but not the Beatles', show.

Before *Sgt. Pepper*, rock music was generally thought of solely as entertain-

ment. But the album made even those from "The Establishment" take rock music

seriously as an intellectual art form. People gathered together to play the album

over and over again to search for songs' hidden meanings and keys to spiritual

AL AGRICULTURAL HALL, ISLINGTON

OPEN XMAS-EVE,
UNTIL FEB, 10TH

LESSEES & MANAGERS,
MESSRS T. READ & F. BAILEY.

WORLD'S FAIR

TO BE SEEN FREE.
GRAND
CIRCUS
AT INTERVALS DAILY

PONCHERY
MONARCH
OF THE HIGH ROPE
TWICE DAILY
WOMBWELL'S Nº 1
MENAGERIE
ALWAYS ON VIEW
PERFORMING LIONS & TRAINED ANI

THE THREE FITZRO
AERIAL FLYING WONDER
TWICE DAILY.

MONKEY HOUSE

LITHO
C. REBER
PLYMOUTH

ADMISSION D.

ADMISSION

John Lennon adapted the song "Being for the Benefit of Mr. Kite" from a circus poster he had bought in an antique shop. To recreate a carnival feel, the studio used recordings of calliopes and fairground organs.

enlightenment. The cover, which featured the Beatles dressed in old military garb and surrounded by cutouts of contemporary cultural and political figures, was a daring design and personified the group spirit and political awareness of the day. It depicted the figures gathered around a plot of dirt topped by the word "Beatles" spelled out in flowers, an image that may be said to mean the band, as Sgt. Pepper's band, was attending its own funeral. Even the back cover of the album was distinctive; it listed the lyrics to all of the songs, something that had never been done before. *Sgt. Pepper*'s design, lyrics, themes, and imagery broke all the rules, paving the way for other bands to do the same.

In 1968, at George Harrison's urging, the Beatles traveled to India to study Eastern music and meditation with famous teacher Maharishi Mahesh Yogi. *Sgt. Pepper* had helped to popularize Eastern music and philosophy among young people.

Wearing buttons (above) was a sign of solidarity in the '60s; the Beatles with the Maharishi in March 1968 (opposite).

In 1969, a rumor circulated that Paul McCartney had died years earlier in a car accident and been replaced by a look-alike. *Life* magazine sent a representative to Great Britain to certify that he was still alive.

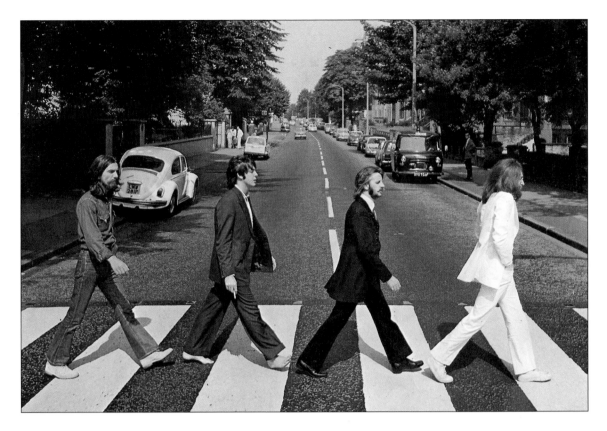

After it was featured on the cover of the Beatles' 12th album, London's Abbey Road became a hugely popular street.

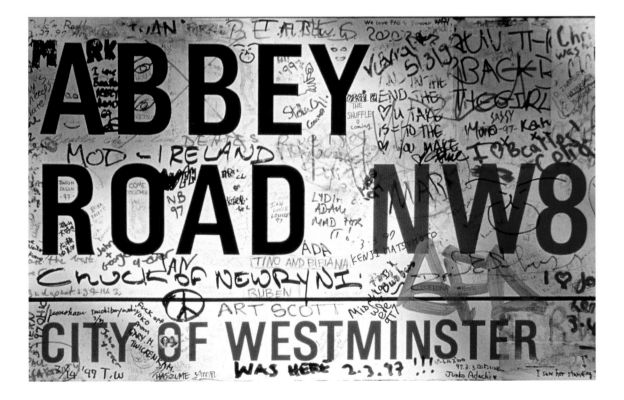

The street sign for Abbey Road is perpetually covered in graffiti from those who want to mark their presence.

After the group's happy times (opposite) were over, Lennon recorded a few albums on his own (above).

Although the Beatles produced five more albums together, none reached the heights

of creativity and artistry that *Sgt. Pepper* did. Some critics derided the *Sgt. Pepper* album

as self-indulgent, but it nevertheless won the Grammy Award for Album of the Year in

1968, becoming the first rock album to do so. By the late 1960s, the peace, love, and

optimism that had characterized the decade and *Sgt. Pepper* itself were disappearing.

The Beatles had reached the end of the road as well and officially broke up

in 1970. However, the legacy of *Sgt. Pepper* lives on, and, with a little help

from today's rockers, it will continue to influence the music of tomorrow.

By 1969, the Beatles had begun to go their separate ways. The Fab Four gave their last public performance that year, a spontaneous, open-air concert on the rooftop of Apple Records in London.

What in the World?

1940–1943	Ringo Starr, John Lennon, Paul McCartney, and George Harrison are born in Liverpool, England.
1941	Japan attacks the U.S. naval base at Pearl Harbor; the U.S. enters World War II.
1945	The first Slinky toy, invented by naval engineer Richard James, hits shelves in Philadelphia, Pennsylvania.
1950	The Diners Club, the first modern credit card, is introduced in New York.
1952	American Jonas Salk creates the polio vaccine, eliminating the disease worldwide.
1954	The U.S. Supreme Court, in *Brown vs. Board of Education*, rules that segregation is unconstitutional.
1956	John Lennon forms a band called The Quarry Men in Liverpool.
1957	Paul McCartney joins The Quarry Men; he introduces George Harrison to the group the following year.
1962	Ringo Starr joins the Beatles; they release "Love Me Do," their first single.
1964	The first Japanese "bullet" train opens, running at speeds of 131 miles (210 km) per hour.
1965	Soviet cosmonaut Aleksei Leonov becomes the first person to walk in space.
1966	Chairman Mao Zedong launches the Cultural Revolution in China to regain control of the Communist Party.
1967	*Sgt. Pepper's Lonely Hearts Club Band* is released and becomes a top seller.
1968	Civil rights activist Martin Luther King Jr. and Senator Robert F. Kennedy are assassinated.
1969	Astronaut Neil Armstrong becomes the first man to walk on the moon.
1969	The children's program *Sesame Street* first airs on public television stations.
1970	The Beatles officially break up and go on to pursue separate musical careers.

Copyright

Published by Creative Education
P.O. Box 227, Mankato, Minnesota 56002

Creative Education is an imprint of The Creative Company.
Design by Rita Marshall
Production design by The Design Lab

Photographs by Alamy (Chris Fredriksson, Tom Hanley, Guy Moberly, The Photolibrary Wales, Photos 12, Pictorial Press Ltd, POPPER-FOTO), Corbis (Andy Warhol Foundation, Geoffrey Clements), Getty Images (Michael Abramson//Time Life Pictures, AFP, Blank Archives, John Downing/Express, Express Newspapers, Hulton Archive, Imagno, Keystone Features, Robert Lackenbach//Time Life Pictures, GERALD LEROUX/AFP, John Loengard/Time Life Pictures, Danny Martindale/WireImage, Stan Meagher/Express, Michael Ochs Archives, Herbert Orth//Time Life Pictures, Cecil Stoughton//Time Life Pictures, Dick Swanson//Time Life Pictures, Time Life Pictures, Donald Uhrbrock, Michael Webb, J. Wilds/Keystone, John Williams/BIPs, JUNG YEON-JE/AFP), iStockphoto (Joe Iera)

Illustration copyright © 2009 Etienne Delessert (10)

Library of Congress Cataloging-in-Publication Data
Wimmer, Teresa.
The Beatles: Sgt. Pepper's Lonely Hearts Club Band / by Teresa Wimmer.
p. cm. — (What in the world?)
Includes index.
ISBN 978-1-58341-651-8
1. Sgt. Pepper's Lonely Hearts Club Band—Juvenile literature. 2. Rock music—1961–1970—Juvenile literature. I. Title. II. Series.

ML3930.B39W56 2008   782.42166092'2—dc22   2007006945

First Edition
9 8 7 6 5 4 3 2 1

Index